Manage Meetings Positively

How to take charge and come up with results

A & C Black • London

© A & C Black Ltd 2006

First published in Great Britain 2006 by
A & C Black Publishers Ltd
38 Soho Square
London W1D 3HB

British Library Cataloguing in Publication Data
A CIP record for this book is available from the British Library.

A & C Black uses paper produced with elemental chlorine-free pulp,
harvested from managed sustainable forests.

ISBN-10: 0–7136–7523–3
ISBN-13: 978–0–7136–7523–8

Design by Fiona Pike, Pike Design, Winchester
Typeset by RefineCatch Limited, Bungay, Suffolk
Printed in Italy by Legoprint

Contents

How do *you* manage meetings?

With so much of your working life spent in meetings, are you really making the best of your time and resources? Answer the questions to find out if you're managing your meetings effectively, and providing strong, structured leadership.

1. When do you call a meeting?
a) First thing every morning, with everyone expected to attend.
b) When key issues will be best sorted out face to face with all the relevant people in attendance.
c) It's usually an ad hoc, last-minute affair.

2. How do you handle difficult situations that arise in meetings?
a) I shout loudest, shout longest.
b) I try to keep maintain balance and control.
c) I'm more your 'passive aggressive' type.

3. How would you approach a meeting with people from a different culture?
a) It's my way or the highway.
b) I'd do some research beforehand to found out some basic rules.
c) I tend to muddle through and keep smiling.

4. How assertive are you?
a) Very, but I think I verge on aggressive at times.
b) Relatively so. I think it's the best way to help others communicate better and to facilitate the best outcome.
c) Not very. Anything for a quiet life.

5. Are you a decisive person?
a) Yes, but I can be a bit hasty.
b) Yes, but I take my time. I try to think through all the options first.
c) I'm not sure.

6. How do you feel about 'virtual' meetings?
a) I wish all my meetings were 'virtual'!
b) They can save a lot of time and money, but there are a few drawbacks.
c) Lukewarm, to say the least.

7. How well do your brainstorming sessions work?
a) They generate lots of ideas, but nothing that sticks.
b) Well. The key is to harness the creativity of your team.
c) They're just not my thing. I prefer more structure.

a = 1, b = 2, c = 3.
Now add up your scores.

- **7–10**: You don't lack strength and authority — or the ability to get results — but your manner and strong-arm tactics could be preventing you from getting the *right* results. Through tact, negotiation, and diplomacy you could bring out the best in your team members. Remember that the point of a meeting is to interact with others, not just to present your opinion. Chapter **4** deals extensively with assertiveness and how to walk the fine line between assertive and aggressive.

■ **11–17**: You seem to have got it just right, providing leadership from the centre, listening and responding well to the demands of managing a meeting. Don't be afraid to put down the management manual once in a while and exercise your own creativity as well as facilitating others'.

■ **18–21**: People are a problem, aren't they? Let your good nature be an asset rather than a burden, by building up your backbone and flexing those key skills that got you the job in the first place. You need some positive structure to strengthen your talents. Read on!

Managing meetings: The basics

Meetings are a necessary evil in everyone's working life. Handled well, they can help those attending to get to the bottom of a tricky situation, agree actions, and do something positive. Handled badly, they can be a terrible waste of time. Basically, you want to get in and out as soon as possible with the relevant decisions made so that you can get on with the rest of your day.

This chapter offers advice for anyone who has to plan and chair a meeting. Special arrangements need to be made for large events such as board meetings or annual general meetings, so in this chapter we focus only on the type of meeting held most commonly in an everyday work situation.

Step one: Decide if you really need a meeting

Meetings are not always a good use of people's time and effort.

✔ If someone suggests that a meeting be held to discuss
    an issue related to your project, team, or department,
    think hard about whether gathering the attendees in
    one place is really the best thing to do.

There may be more efficient alternatives. For example, you
could try:

■ Conference calls or videoconferencing. If you have
    access to these facilities, or can afford to use or
    acquire them, they offer a good way of holding a
    discussion without having to disrupt the attendees'
    day too much.
■ E-mail. You could send a message to all relevant parties,
    setting out the issue clearly, asking for a response, and
    giving a deadline. Double-check that you have included
    everyone before sending it.

If all else fails, though, and a face-to-face meeting seems to
be the best and least unwieldy way of agreeing action on the
issue at hand, prepare as much as you can in advance and
delegate where appropriate.

TOP TIP
Think carefully about the type of meeting
you need. Brainstorming sessions or
creative discussions don't fit easily into
well-planned timetables, so may be
best slotted into less hectic times
of the week, month, or year.

Step two: Do the initial planning

1 Think carefully about who to invite

To avoid wasting time and money, try to limit numbers by inviting only those who *really* need to be at the meeting. These will be people directly involved in decisions that must be taken, those significantly affected by any actions, or those who have some specific knowledge to contribute.

✔ The most productive meetings are usually those with the least number of people attending. If the agenda is lengthy and covers a variety of issues, consider asking people to drop in and out when their relevant topic comes up for discussion.

2 Give the attendees all relevant information in good time

✔ To make sure that all attendees have a chance to raise their concerns during the meeting, give them plenty of notice of the time and venue, and circulate a draft agenda outlining the topics to be discussed, as well as the time limits assigned to each topic.

TOP TIP
It is vital that all attendees are clear about the purpose of the meeting and why they have been called together. The agenda

---

**should set out what needs to be
accomplished between the start
and finish of the meeting.**

Time limits create a healthy sense of urgency. By stipulating the start and finish time of the meeting, as well as setting limits for each topic on the agenda (particularly important if you are holding a lengthy meeting and asking people to drop in and out), you will encourage people to stay focused. For this to work, of course, it is essential to stick to these times!

Other information you should provide your attendees with prior to the meeting includes:

- directions to the venue, in case they haven't been there before
- information about those attending (particularly helpful if you are going to be joined by people external to your company, such as consultants, freelance contributors, or designers)
- relevant background information or documents. For example, if you are going to discuss a long-overdue revamp of your product catalogue, send everyone a copy of your existing brochure. You could also include other similar publications which you admire, to help people come up with new ideas for presenting your products
- your contact details and those of one other person in the office (such as your assistant, if you have one) in case of emergency

3 Think about catering requirements

✔ If you think your meeting will take longer than a few hours, or is likely to take place over lunch, remember to ask all attendees whether they have any special dietary requirements. This will save a lot of time and stress on the day.

TOP TIP
Research shows that the best time to hold a meeting is just before lunch or towards the end of the day. This motivates everyone to focus on the agenda and keep to time!

---

4 Delegate taking the minutes

Try to find someone other than yourself to take the minutes. This will free you up to steer the meeting as appropriate.

✔ If the person designated as the minute-taker is new to the project or issue under discussion, run through any key words or acronyms that are likely to arise so that he or she is not baffled by the jargon. You and the other attendees may be well versed in the relevant vocabulary, but don't expect the same from a 'newcomer'.

Do make sure, though, that the minute-taker knows the names of all attendees.

Step three: Find and prepare the venue

✔ Once you know that a formal meeting is on the cards, find an appropriate space in which it can be held. Some companies have a 'booking system' for meeting rooms, so give yourself enough time when planning the time and date to ensure that you can get a suitably sized room. Don't just assume it'll be free as and when you're ready!

✔ Give yourself plenty of time to prepare the room as the meeting gets closer. In particular make sure that:

- the room is tidy
- you have enough tables and chairs to accommodate everyone
- the flip chart, if you're using one, has enough paper and pens ready
- there is sufficient light, heating, or ventilation for the time of day and year
- there are enough power points, and that they're in the right place if you are going to be using an overhead projector or laptop
- any equipment in the room is ready to use and is working properly

✔ Make catering arrangements, once your numbers are confirmed. If your company has a canteen, book in early for someone to bring water, tea, coffee, and biscuits to the meeting. If you don't have a canteen, ask a colleague or assistant to stay close by at the start of the meeting and to pop out to a nearby coffee shop or café to fetch what is needed. Again, this will free you up to attend to other tasks.

TOP TIP

Think carefully about the seating plan. If the meeting is informal, sitting together at a round table—so that there is no hierarchy—is a good plan. For more formal gatherings, the chair should sit at the head of the table. If it's likely that the meeting will be highly charged or argumentative, or if you know that some participants just don't get on, make sure they sit on opposite sides of the table. It won't guarantee that they will agree, but they will be able to see each other's facial expressions and body language, both of which are important.

Step four: Keep on track

1 Start as you mean to go on

On the day of the meeting, arrive in plenty of time so that you can double-check that everything is ready. Once the attendees have arrived, set the pace and tone of the meeting by following these steps:

✓ Begin on time. (Make sure you can see an accurate clock from where you're sitting.)

✓ Welcome everyone, and briefly explain basic issues such as where the bathrooms are located (particularly helpful for anyone who hasn't been to your offices before) and what the catering arrangements are.

✓ Ask everyone to check that they've turned off their mobile phones so that the flow of discussion isn't interrupted.

✓ Reiterate the reason the meeting is being held, what you hope to achieve within the meeting, the time-scale, and the finishing time.

✓ Frame each item on the agenda by explaining its objectives.

2 Keep a tight rein on proceedings

While obviously you need to give everyone an opportunity to contribute to points raised on the agenda, there are steps you can take to make sure that you keep roughly on schedule (and on topic).

✓ Make sure that attendees keep to one agenda point at a time.

✓ Firmly but politely move the discussion on if a subject has become exhausted.

TOP TIP
Sometimes meetings aren't as creative as
you may have hoped, and ideas can dry up.
If the focus of your meeting is to
brainstorm an idea or problem, you
may need to kickstart the
conversation. See Chapter 7
for detailed advice.

✔ Don't let one person dominate the conversation.
Meetings can often be hijacked by one or two vociferous
attendees, so in your role as chair you need to have
some strategies to deal with people like this so
that everyone can have a fair say, and so that you
keep to schedule. See Chapter 2 for more information
on this.

✔ Look around the table to see if people are actively trying
to get your attention, say by raising their hand or a pen.
Watch out for positive body language that shows
people are attentive, engaged, and want to have
their say.

✔ Make sure that there is only one discussion at a time.
Meetings often get sidetracked when some attendees
start their own 'private' debate during the main session.
This may range from a few whispered asides, or notes
being passed around the table, to a full-blown separate

discussion taking place. You will never finish the
main meeting on time if you allow this to happen,
so interrupt these diversions by addressing the
people involved directly and asking them if there's
something they'd like to raise. For example, you
could say: 'I think there may be an issue you're not
happy with. Would you like to raise it now before
we go any further? We have a lot to get through
today.' Be assertive not aggressive, polite but
firm.

✔ Summarise at appropriate intervals and restate agreed
action points clearly (the person taking the minutes will
be particularly grateful for this).

✔ Wrap up the meeting by thanking everyone for their
attendance and contribution. If possible, also let
attendees know when the next meeting is to be held
(should you need one). This will not only save time on
e-mails and phone calls but, by giving a sense of
continuity and progress, will encourage people not to
forget what has been discussed the moment they
leave the room.

Step five: Make sure everyone is clear on any follow-up action required

✔ Ask the person taking the minutes to write them up as soon as possible so that they can be distributed to all the attendees promptly.

Bear in mind that most of the attendees will only glance briefly at the meeting minutes, or refer back to them in order to locate a specific piece of information. This means that they need to be extremely concise and clear. The key things to note are:

- agreed actions
- the people responsible for them
- deadline (if appropriate)
- date of next meeting, if you agreed to arrange another

Common mistakes

✗ **You leave preparations to the last minute**

You're not saving time by leaving the arrangements for your meeting to the last minute—you're wasting it. The sooner you get started the better, as it will save you panicking on the day itself about exactly how many people are coming, whether you can cater for them all, where your laptop can be plugged in, and other myriad potential nightmares. If you plan in advance, you can make sure everything is in place early and spend the time you'd waste by rushing about doing something more productive instead.

✗ You think you can squeeze in taking the minutes

You're not shirking responsibility if you ask someone else to take the meeting's minutes for you. On the contrary, if you are free to make sure that the meeting starts and ends on time, is well organised, and achieves its objectives, you'll have made everyone's life a lot easier, You'll also end up with a set of minutes (and notes) that mean something.

✗ You lose track of time

Don't be afraid to move things on as appropriate if the meeting seems to be getting bogged down in one particular area. Everyone else will be keen to finish on time and get on with the rest of their day, so, in your role as chair, shape the discussion and sustain the meeting's impetus.

STEPS TO SUCCESS

✔ Only call a meeting if you think one is absolutely necessary.

✔ If a meeting does need to be called, give all attendees as much notice as you can.

✔ Give yourself plenty of time to book the venue and arrange the necessary catering and equipment.

✔ Prepare yourself properly and look over the meeting objectives in advance.

✔ On the day of the meeting, arrive on time and begin the meeting punctually.

✔ Make sure only one discussion is happening at any one time in the room.

✔ Give everyone an opportunity to get his or her point across and don't let the conversation be 'hijacked' by one person.

✔ Recap action points so that the person taking the minutes is able to note them easily.

✔ Keep an eye on the clock and move the meeting on if the attendees are becoming stuck on one particular item.

✔ Make sure minutes are circulated promptly after the meeting so that everyone is aware of what is meant to be done, when, and by whom.

Useful links

it-analysis.com:

www.it-analysis.com/article.php?articleid=3728

www.it-analysis.com/article.php?articleid=3729

Meeting Wizard:

www.meetingwizard.org

Vista—Virtual Meetings:

www.vista.uk.com/whatwedolargegroups/

virtualmeetings.php

Coping in difficult meetings

However much planning and preparation you do beforehand, you'll occasionally run into difficulties during meetings—particularly those which involve delicate negotiations. The number of potential problems is legion, but the most common ones fall into two categories: difficult people and difficult situations.

Whether you're chairing or participating in a potentially fraught meeting or negotiation, this chapter will help you find some practical solutions that could break a deadlock or improve a tense atmosphere.

Step one: Deal with difficult people

People are difficult for several reasons. They may have unresolved issues in their personal lives that affect their attitudes and commitment to the subject of the meeting; they may lack empathy and make insensitive or inappropriate remarks, or they may simply be unskilled in negotiating and make mistakes. Whatever the cause, try not to over-react and make the situation worse. Be assured that there are a number of things you can do to move the meeting on in a positive way.

I React appropriately

The difficulties you may encounter with people usually fall into one of a few categories. Someone at a meeting may talk too much; another may feel very strongly about the subject under discussion; a third may become angry. Here are some simple techniques for managing each kind of situation.

- **The talkative**—In the case of people who just like the sound of their own voice, you must be assertive enough to interject politely but firmly and remind everyone of the agenda point you're discussing and steer the discussion back to it. Also mention your target finish time and how the meeting is progressing in relation to it.
- **The passionate**—The same goes for dealing with people who feel very strongly about the issue under discussion and who may feel that others do not share their interest and commitment. Again, make sure that they get the opportunity to voice their point of view, but also that they give others the chance to express theirs too. Interject as appropriate and summarise if you sense they are about to repeat something. Remember that a meeting is a discussion with objectives, not an opportunity for attendees to rehearse an extended monologue.
- **The angry**—If the topic you are discussing is particularly contentious, tempers may flare. If you feel a situation is getting heated and that insults rather

than well-considered opinions are being traded, step
in to defuse the tension. Suggest a break outside
the meeting room for 15 minutes or so, which will give
most people time to calm down and assess what has
happened. If voices are being raised, match your
voice to the level of other people's, then reduce the
volume back down to a normal speaking pitch. This
will allow the discussion to get back to a more stable
footing.

2 Manage your own behaviour

When faced with people being difficult in a meeting that
you are managing, it can be easy to get too involved, to the
extent where you begin to be difficult yourself. For this
reason, it is worth trying to make a calm decision on how
you are going to behave. Essentially, you have two
choices—as illustrated in the diagram below.

Source: Margerison

✔ **Solution-centred behaviour.** When someone asks us for help, or appears to need it, the natural tendency of most people is to try to offer a solution. We generally produce one of the three reactions in the top half of the diagram:

- we advise people what to do
- we tell them what to do
- we offer to do something for them under certain conditions

This is called 'solution-centred behaviour' because it focuses principally on finding an answer. Sometimes this works, but it is rather easy to produce a brilliant solution to what later turns out to be the wrong problem. And when this happens, it is, of course, your fault!

✔ **Problem-centred behaviour.** This means going 'below the line' shown in the diagram, and questioning the other person about how he or she understands the problem.

You can do this either by **consulting** ('what exactly is the problem?', 'when did it occur?', 'what might have caused it?', and so on) or **reflecting** ('I can see that you're very angry about this, what's causing it?', 'what aspect of the problem is troubling you most?'). The key message here is to consult about **facts** and reflect on **feelings**.

The purpose is to make sure that you both share a clear understanding of what the problem is. In fact, helping the other person to clarify his or her thinking about the problem often allows the answer to emerge as if by magic. The other party then feels as if he or she 'owns' the solution—and is therefore committed to it—and you may not need to use the solution-centred behaviour at all. Even if the answer does not appear automatically, you can now direct or advise from a much better understanding of the issues.

Listen!

Some people become angry, difficult, or distressed if they think they're being ignored. Active listening is a very useful skill that you can use in these situations to build rapport and also to make the other person feel involved. It can also yield valuable information that could help a meeting run much more smoothly.

Active listening is about demonstrating that you have understood and are interested in what is being said. It requires good eye contact, lots of head nods, and responses such as 'Ah ha', 'Mmmm', and 'I understand what you mean'. In addition, a good active listener summarises what has been said to demonstrate his or her understanding, and asks open questions such as, 'Can you tell me more about . . .?' and 'What do you think . . .?'. These questions encourage further communication and enrich what is being communicated.

3 Tap into the power of questions

The key to the 'below-the-line' approach is that it obliges you to ask questions. This is always a good idea if you have to deal with difficult people, as it enables you to control the conversation—if you ask a question, people will usually answer it. This approach avoids confrontation, and it may get you valuable information about the person or the negotiation.

4 Remember the guidelines

✔ When in doubt, go 'below the line' and consult and reflect.

✔ Ask good, useful, open questions: plan them carefully.

✔ Ask for the other party's proposals or ideas—don't give yours first.

✔ Ask for clarification of the other person's proposals, rather than saying what is wrong with them.

✔ Ask about their goals and objectives rather than telling them about yours.

✔ Ask how you can help them.

TOP TIP
**Be subtle! If the other person spots what
is going on, he or she might feel
manipulated—so keep your
questioning within reasonable limits.**

5 Have a back-up plan

If the other person is still being 'difficult' and hindering the meeting's progress, more drastic action is needed. Either he or she doesn't want a conclusion to be reached, or is unable to conduct the discussion properly at this time. In any case, you need to do something to move things along.

✔ Acknowledge that there seems to be a problem.

✔ Ask three key questions:

- Does he or she want to continue the discussions?

- Would it be better if you spoke with someone else? A more senior member of staff, for example?

- Is there anything you can do that will help him or her feel more comfortable with the negotiation?

Step two: Deal with difficult situations

It's almost impossible to guess the many potential problems that could crop up in a meeting, but in this section we list some common fraught issues.

1 The topic under discussion is controversial

It's a good idea to start working on this problem even before the meeting starts. Find out as much as you can about the issue, from both sides, so that you are prepared well in advance. If the issue is particularly complex, make notes that you can refer to. Use the tactics mentioned above and below if feelings begin to run high.

2 You know for a fact that at least two attendees have a bad working relationship

Again, put in some work well ahead of the meeting so that you won't be walking in cold to a difficult situation. If you're chairing an internal meeting, it's likely that you'll know most of the people there, what they're like, how they interact with others, and any fraught relationships they may have. If the meeting involves external parties, you may not know what the dynamic is, but again, some research will help. Ask colleagues who do know the other invitees to give you the low-down on them so that if any tension does emerge, you're not taken by surprise.

TOP TIP

Watching participants' body language is another good way of keeping tabs on a difficult situation and on whether it might be on the point of exploding. Facial expressions are generally—but not always—the best indication of how someone is feeling, but people often bluff. However, their body language can often let them down if it doesn't match their facial expressions. Watch for signs of someone becoming tense or angry: this could include folding their arms and pushing themselves

---

**away from the table, as if to 'disengage' from
the proceedings. Are there any nervous
laughs? Raised eyebrows?**

Whatever the background, though, be ready to act if some
participants start to argue.

■ Keep calm yourself.
■ As mentioned above, don't raise your voice unless other
people are shouting and you need to match their volume:
once you have their attention, bring your voice back
down to a normal speaking level.
■ 'Flush out' poor behaviour: if someone is sighing loudly
when someone else speaks, for example, making
asides, murmuring 'rubbish' under their breath or some
such, call a halt to proceedings, make it clear you have
noticed what is going on and ask him or her to explain
what is happening.
■ Remind participants of why you are having the meeting
at all, and what you want to achieve.
■ If the person—or people—involved in a tense exchange
can't modify their behaviour, call a halt for five minutes. If,
when the meeting resumes, things are no better, it may
be better to end the meeting itself than struggle on.

TOP TIP
**Even if you feel more sympathy for one
person's point of view than another, if you are
chairing a meeting you must remain impartial
at all times. You are there to facilitate an**

open exchange of views, not impose your own
preferred outcome. Make sure that everyone
has a chance to speak and encourage
compromise and concessions on both sides,
where possible: that will avoid one party
feeling that they have given all the ground
and gained nothing in response.

3 You feel the meeting is being 'ambushed'

For a variety of reasons, people may at times try to make a
meeting fail completely. They may not like the way it is going,
feel aggrieved at having to be there at all, or feel that it is
unnecessary, for example. Whatever, the reason, act quickly
to stop this disruptive behaviour. Be vocal about the fact that
you have spotted this tactic and that you are not going to let
it succeed. Ask the person to amend his or her behaviour or
leave, and be ready to enforce the latter option if he or she
doesn't start to act more positively.

Common mistakes

✗ You don't get to the bottom of why someone is being 'difficult'

Even though your patience may be stretched to its
absolute limit, try to put yourself in the other party's
shoes to find out why they are acting in the way that they
are. Also ask questions that allow the other party to
disclose their concerns and motivations—you may

actually be able to help them, thus achieving that ideal win/win goal.

✗ You battle on when it's just not worth it

While everyone aims to tie up negotiations with the least amount of fuss and wasted time possible, some days it just won't work. On those occasions, it's important to recognise this, cut your losses, and rearrange for another time.

STEPS TO SUCCESS

✔ Work out whether the situation is worth saving.

✔ If things have gone too far, consider postponing the meeting to another day.

✔ If it is worth carrying on, try to work out whether solution-based or problem-based behaviour will help salvage the discussion.

✔ Ask useful, 'open' questions that allow the other party to respond fully and convey to you why they are being 'difficult'.

✔ Ask for the other party's views and ideas.

✔ Be subtle!

✔ Have a back-up plan.

✔ If you are chairing a meeting about a contentious issue, do as much research as you can beforehand to find out about both sides of the argument.

✔ Try to discover as much as you can about the dynamics of the group in the meeting. It will help you head off potential conflict.

✔ Watch out for people's body language, as well as their facial expressions, to give you a clue of how they really feel about something.

✔ Stay impartial, whatever your personal views on a given subject.

Useful links

The Negotiation Skills Company:
www.negotiationskills.com/articles.html
Work911.com:
www.work911.com/cgi-bin/links/jump.cgi?ID=3323

Meeting with people from other cultures

With business becoming 'global' and increasing numbers of international mergers and acquisitions taking place, it probably won't be long before you find yourself holding meetings with people from other cultures. Going abroad to seek new customers or business partners is the obvious example, but receiving potential clients or suppliers from overseas or even doing business with other parts of your own company— if it's multinational—will involve you in cross-cultural negotiations.

Remember that it's not up to the other person to adapt to you; *not* attempting to understand and take account of the other party's cultural background may be received as an insult. On the other hand, most people *will* notice if you make the effort and give you generous credit for it.

The best way to prepare for cross-cultural meetings is by living in the other culture, or by finding a reliable local mentor or partner. Clearly this isn't always possible, but there are things that you can do to improve the probability of success and minimise the risk of mistakes. Careful planning and attention will pay dividends.

Step one: Investigate social conventions

Wherever you're travelling to on your business trip, finding out more about the social conventions of a country or region is invaluable.

Obvious differences in cultural style are easy to spot, but it's the more subtle distinctions that usually cause problems. For example, unintended rudeness or failure to observe little politenesses can quickly make negotiations awkward. These subtleties usually occur in a small number of general situations, so observe these carefully when you're in the country, and investigate them as much as you can beforehand.

1 Meeting and greeting procedures

Watch how these work. For example, you need to think about:

- who introduces whom
- whether gestures such as bowing are appropriate
- whether you're expected to shake hands and, if so, how
- whether women shake hands
- whether there are set greetings and responses

✔ As a general rule, hold back. It's wise to be guided by your hosts and avoid any physical contact until you're sure it's acceptable. Also, don't be too enthusiastic in adopting local customs — it may make some people suspect that you're mimicking them, rather than trying to match your approach to fit theirs.

Watch your (body) language!

Remember that a lot of the non-verbal clues we give to colleagues or friends when we communicate with them don't always travel very well to other countries. While a smile can rarely go wrong, bear in mind that some cultures:

- find the 'ok' sign offensive (that is, thumb and forefinger closed together to make a circle)
- find the 'thumbs up' sign offensive
- use a nod of the head to mean 'no' and a shake of the head to mean 'yes'
- think that standing with hands on hips means that someone is angry
- are less offended by a lack of personal space than others — for example, people may stand right up close while talking to you; disconcerting if you're not expecting it
- prefer a kiss on both cheeks to a handshake
- value silence more than people do in the West — in Japan, for example, silences during a conversation are important and designate 'thinking time'. Talking too much during a negotiation is thus a bad move; say only what you really need to

- are reluctant to make eye contact—in some Latin American and African countries, particularly, this can be seen as insulting
- get to the point more quickly than others—in some countries, long, circular discussions may all be part of negotiations. These may drive you mad if you're in a rush; you need to be patient and adjust to a different pace of life—avoid arranging back-to-back meetings in these cultures
- are offended by people who chew gum or keep their hands in their pockets during conversations
- are much more tactile than others
- won't sit with their legs crossed, as this may mean that the sole of their shoe is pointing at someone, which can be considered extremely rude

2 Ideas about time

Observe local customs about timing of meetings, particularly:

- The rules about appointments: do you turn up *on* time (Europe); *before* time (China); or a little *after* time (Africa)?
- How time is used, rigidly or flexibly: does a half-hour appointment mean exactly 30 minutes, or anything up to an hour?
- How your host will indicate that your time is up: how and when can you politely take your leave?

3 The role of women

Some cultures have embraced the role of women in
business more than others, and may have very clear
conventions governing gender relationships. You need
to know:

- how women's role is defined in the country you're
  visiting. Don't comment on this, whatever your views
  may be
- what roles women play in business
- any 'rules' covering relationships between men and
  women at work and socially

4 Eating and drinking etiquette

In many cultures, eating with others has symbolism and
rituals that can be culturally very sensitive. Sometimes these
are based on religion, sometimes on historical tradition. If
you're invited to a meal, find out beforehand from a reliable
source what the etiquette is, particularly:

- what form the meal will take, that is, whether it's formal
  or informal
- customs such as washing, which hand to use when
  eating, formal ceremonies, if there are prayers before
  meals, and so on
- what people normally drink with their food, that is,
  whether alcohol is permissible or not
- whether it is polite to eat/drink everything, or whether
  you should leave something on your plate

- whether business is discussed over meals
- any dress conventions

TOP TIP
Watch what others do and be guided by them.
Don't be offended if people lean over and
help themselves from your plate—this
is polite in some cultures!

---

5 Gifts

This can be a sensitive area: some cultures will tend to perceive a gift as a bribe, others as an embarrassment. Therefore, find out:

- what is the attitude to gifts—are they accepted or expected?
- the type of gift that is appropriate. Be particularly careful about gifts to your host or hostess if invited to someone's home
- customs for receiving gifts yourself

This is one of those areas where no-one will notice if you get it right, but everyone will be aware if you get something wrong!

6 Humour

Don't make jokes until you are sure you understand the jokes made by the people you're with! Be aware that irony and sarcasm often aren't recognised easily by people who don't share your first language, so don't take refuge in either of them too much.

If the worst comes to the worst and you feel you've made a gaffe, don't try to 'rescue' the situation by making another joke. It's best just to move on and pick up the threads of your earlier conversation, or start a new one.

Step two: Understand business practices

Although there's increasingly a common core to ways of doing business internationally, there are certain important conventions and habits that distinguish one culture's way of doing business from another. If you're working in new markets, you must be able to answer the questions below. Get help or advice if you can't; guesswork isn't recommended.

I National characteristics

Since the end of the Cold War, many new countries have been created and new markets opened up for business. Some of these countries have no recent history of dealing with overseas clients and little experience of international trade, so doing business there can be tough. But forewarned is forearmed: find out what you can about cultural attitudes in the country you are visiting and be ready to deal with them patiently. Look particularly at:

- the country's understanding and acceptance of outsiders
- who controls business and how it works
- how decisions are made: is the culture one where compromise is sought, or is it more competitive?
- how the country's legal, technical, and financial systems differ from your own; are there any special conditions that will have to be met?
- whether support systems (transport, banking arrangements, and so on) are adequate to deliver the deal, and whether the party you're doing business with has reasonable control of them

2 Language

If your meeting is more of a negotiation than a straightforward 'getting to know you' session, negotiate in your own language if you can. Fluency gives power, but be aware that the other side has already made a concession to you!

✔ Don't underestimate the dangers of missing subtle points when you have to work in another language. Use this to your advantage: slow things down and ask for clarification frequently.

✔ In most cultures you will 'gain points' for speaking their language—but many will be less forgiving of 'cultural errors' if you do. You might decide not to disclose your knowledge of their language if it isn't fluent.

✓ Confirm all concessions: check for accidental misunderstandings.

✓ If you work in your own language, check regularly that the other party has understood you properly. Use questions or summaries to do this.

3 Working with an interpreter

If you feel it's appropriate, employ an interpreter. Make sure that he or she:

- is professionally neutral and properly skilled
- understands what negotiating is about and what the objectives are
- can translate not just words but also meanings through gestures, tone, and so on

✓ Rehearse with your interpreter to create familiarity with likely scenarios.

✓ Don't accept the other party's interpreter if the negotiation is an important one.

✓ Plan plenty of breaks: long negotiations in a foreign setting are very tiring.

✓ Remember to summarise any points that are agreed before moving onto new topics for discussion.

Step three: Keep the basics in mind

✔ Don't be in too much of a hurry. Give yourself plenty of time to deal with the unexpected, to recover from travel, to get used to the climate, and so on.

✔ Decide under whose law contracts will be drawn up (preferably your own). If you have to accept the other party's law, check out the implications carefully.

✔ Be sure that technical, professional, safety, and environmental standards accord with the other party's national standards, and are acceptable to your own organisation.

✔ Make sure you've established a good line of communication with your home base.

✔ Don't try to take on the style of the other culture. Be aware of it, but retain your own (cultural) style and play to your strengths.

Common mistakes

✗ You think you can wing it

Taking the time to find out more about another culture may seem like a bind, but any preparation you do will come in very useful. Imagine how embarrassed you'd be if a negotiation came to nothing because of a gauche remark or gesture you made. Courtesy is essential in business: you would expect it of others, and they will expect it of you.

✗ You try to cover uncertainty with jokes

Remember that some jokes just won't work when translated into another language, and may make things worse if a situation is getting heated. Everything may be fine if you know your opposite party well, but err on the side of caution if you're meeting someone for the first time, or if the negotiation is particularly fraught.

STEPS TO SUCCESS

✔ If you're negotiating abroad or with others from a different culture, find out as much as you can about their way of doing things beforehand, or find someone who can help you.

✔ Observe meeting and greeting conventions.

✔ Watch your body language as well as your verbal communication.

✔ Investigate eating and drinking etiquette in case you're invited for a meal.

✔ Be very careful if offering a gift to the other party.

Negotiate in your own first language if you can. If not, hire an impartial interpreter.

Useful links

BusinessCulture.com:
www.businessculture.com
Business Know-How:
www.businessknowhow.com/growth/body-language.htm
ExecutivePlanet.com:
www.executiveplanet.com

Communicating assertively during meetings

Whether you're chairing a meeting or participating in one that's important to you, communicating assertively will help you get your point across and keep control.

Assertiveness is an approach to communication that honours your own choices, as well as those of the person you are communicating with. It is not about being aggressive and steamrollering other viewpoints, but about seeking and exchanging opinions, developing a full understanding of the issues, and negotiating a win–win outcome.

To assess your level of assertiveness, ask youself:

- Do you feel 'put upon' or ignored in your exchanges with colleagues?
- Are you unable to speak your mind and ask for what you want?
- Do you find it difficult to stand up for yourself in a discussion?
- Are you inordinately grateful when someone seeks your opinion and takes it into account?

If you answer 'yes' to most of these questions, you may need to consider becoming more assertive.

Step one: Choose the right approach

Becoming assertive is all about making choices that meet your needs and the needs of the situation. Sometimes it is appropriate to be passive. If you were facing a snarling dog, you might not want to provoke an attack by looking for a win–win outcome! There may be other occasions when aggression is the answer. However, this is still assertive behaviour as *you*, rather than other people or situations, are in control of how you react.

TOP TIP

After a lifetime of being the way they are, some people are daunted by the prospect of change. But if you don't change what you do, you'll never change what you get. All it takes to change is a decision. Once you have made that decision, you will naturally observe yourself in situations, notice what you do and don't do well, and then you can try out new behaviours to see what works for you.

✔ You may find it helpful to investigate specially tailored training courses so that you can try out some approaches before taking on a colleague or manager in a 'live' situation. This sort of thing takes practice.

Step two: Practise projecting a positive image

✔ Use 'winning' language. Rather than saying 'I always come off worst', say 'I've learned a great deal from doing lots of different things in my career. I'm now ready to move on'. This is the beginning of taking control in your life.

✔ Visualise what you wish to become; make the image as real as possible, and feel the sensation of being in control. Perhaps there have been moments in your life when you naturally felt like this, a time when you have excelled. Recapture that moment and 'live' it again. Imagine how it would be if you felt like that in other areas of your life. Determine to make this your goal and recall this powerful image or feeling when you are getting disheartened. It will re-energise you and get you back on a positive track.

TOP TIP

If you're not very tall, it's easy to think you can't have presence because people will overlook you. But many of the most successful people, in all areas of life, are

---

physically quite small. Adopting an assertive communication style and body language has the effect of making you look and feel more imposing. Assume you have impact, visualise it, feel it, breathe it.

Step three: Condition others to take you seriously

This can be done through non-verbal as well as verbal communication, and can be particularly effective in a meeting environment.

✓ If someone is talking over you during a meeting and you are finding it difficult to get a word in edgeways, you can hold up your hand signalling 'stop' as you begin to speak. 'I hear what you are saying but I would like to put forward an alternative viewpoint . . .'

✓ Always take responsibility for your communication. Use the 'I' word. 'I would like . . .', 'I don't agree . . .', 'I am uncomfortable with this . . .'

✓ Being aware of non-verbal communication signals can also help you build rapport. If you mirror what others are doing as they communicate with you, it will help you get a sense of where they are coming from and how to respond in the most helpful way. Subtly adopting someone's body language also helps to put him or her at ease.

TOP TIP
Until you get used to being assertive, you may
find it hard to say 'no' to people. One useful
technique is to say, 'I'd like to think about this
first. I'll get back to you shortly'. Giving
yourself time and space to rehearse your
response can be really helpful.

Step four: Use positive body language

✔ Sit up straight, breathe deeply, and look people in the eye when you speak to them.

✔ Instead of anticipating a negative outcome, expect something positive.

✔ Listen actively to the other party and try putting yourself in their shoes so that you have a better chance of seeking the solution that ultimately works for you both.

✔ Inquire about their thoughts and feelings by using 'open' questions, that allow them to give you a full response rather than just 'yes' or 'no'. Examples include: 'Tell me more about why . . .', 'How do you see this working out?', and so forth.

✔ Don't let people talk down to you when you're sitting down. If they're standing, stand up too.

Step five: Recognise different communication styles

There are four types of communication style:

■ **assertive**—where everyone wins
■ **passive/aggressive**—where you lose and do everything you can (without being too obvious) to make others lose too
■ **passive**—where you lose and everyone else wins
■ **aggressive**—where you win and everyone else loses

It's important to appreciate that people communicate in a variety of ways. Your assertiveness therefore needs to be sensitive to a range of possible responses that you might encounter in meetings. Here are some tips on how to deal with the different communication styles outlined above.

✔ **Passive/aggressive people.** If you are dealing with someone behaving in a passive/aggressive manner, you can handle it by exposing what he or she is doing. Try saying things like 'I get the feeling you are not happy about this decision', or 'It appears you have something to say on this; would you like to share your views now?' In this way, they either have to deny their passive/ aggressive stance or they have to disclose their motivations. Either way, you are left in the driving seat.

✔ **Passive people.** If you are dealing with a passive person, rather than let them be silent, encourage them to contribute so that they can't put the blame for their disquiet on someone else.

✔ **Aggressive people.** The aggressive communicator may need confronting, but do it carefully; you don't want things to escalate out of control. Using the 'I'd like to think about it first' technique is often useful in this instance. The main thing to remember is that you have an equal right to be taken into account, including the right to say 'no'. Remember this when you are feeling badgered or defeated by someone.

Conflict is notorious for bringing out aggression in people. However, it is still possible to be assertive in this context. You may need to show that you are taking the aggressive person seriously by reflecting their energy. To do this, you could raise your voice to match the volume of theirs, then bring the volume down as you start to explore what would lead to a win–win solution. 'I CAN SEE THAT YOU ARE UPSET and I would feel exactly the same if I were you . . . however . . .' Then you can establish the desired outcome for both of you.

If you become more assertive, people won't necessarily think that you have become more aggressive. Be responsive to their communication styles, and their needs will be met too. All that will happen is that your communication style becomes more effective.

Common mistakes

✗ You go too far at first

Many people, when trying out assertive behaviour for the first time, find that they go too far and become aggressive. An important meeting with a new client or a potentially tense encounter with a disgruntled customer may not be the best place to try out the 'new you'. Remember that you are looking for a win–win, not a you-win-and-they-lose, outcome. Take your time, practise, and ask for feedback from trusted friends or colleagues.

STEPS TO SUCCESS

✓ Speaking positively and using positive body language will encourage others to take you seriously.

✓ In any business situation, and in meetings in particular, it's important to listen carefully to other people so you are clear about which points you differ over, and upon which you agree.

✓ Try your techniques out in a 'safe' environment until you feel comfortable with them. For example, see how you get on in a routine internal meeting before trying out the 'new you' in an important external situation.

Build up a toolkit of assertive techniques and responses that have worked for you in the past and re-use them.

Useful links

Assertiveness.com:
www.assertiveness.com
Assertiveness tip sheet, Tufts University:
www.tufts.edu/hr/tips/assert.html
The Oak Tree Counseling Self-Help Assertiveness Quiz:
www.counseling.com/assrtquz.htm

Making decisions
in meetings

A meeting should be the perfect opportunity to
get decisions made. However, some people are
naturally more decisive than others; for them, it
is relatively easy to respond to a situation, weigh
up how to tackle it, make the decision, and move
on. For the indecisive, the process can be
nightmarish, stressful, and eat up an awful lot
of valuable time.

The trick is to find a decision-making style that
gives you enough time to ensure that a decision is
well considered, but cuts out the procrastination.
Avoid the temptation to make knee-jerk
judgments: you may think you are creating a good
impression by looking decisive, but it is the
quality of the decision that counts in the end.

This chapter aims to help you if you find decision-
making a challenge. While you may not always be
able to predict or control circumstances and,
clearly, some decisions are a lot easier to make
than others, there are skills you can learn that
will improve how you respond. As you practise
these skills, they will gradually become second
nature. The result will be less stress, more
decisiveness, less time wasted, and more focus
in your working life.

**To make the best decision possible, be clear
about your goals, the problem in question, the
options open to you, the possible consequences,
the timescale, and the outcome of previous
decisions on the matter. The process combines
your intuition (to initiate your response and come
up with innovative options) and your analytical
ability (with which you scrutinise and quantify
your options).**

Step one: Understand what you want your decision to achieve

When you are faced with a difficult issue, try to look past
your immediate objective and take in your longer-term
goals as well. For example, say you work in sales and have
dealings with a wide variety of customers. If one of your
customers wants you to drop your price to an
uneconomical level, think about how important the sale is
in the long run. If that customer does not feature in your
business priorities, then you might only damage your
reputation among competitors and other customers by
dropping your price too low. On the other hand, if the
customer is in a sector that you want to break in to, then a
low-margin sale may give you an important foot in the door
for future business.

✔ Once you have defined the objectives of your decision,
you are in a position to determine its level of significance.

This is important when deciding on the amount of time and resources you should spend in making the right decision.

Different decision levels

1 Strategic

Decisions about strategy are concerned with long-term goals, philosophies, and the overall direction of the business. They therefore tend to be more theoretical than practical, more unpredictable in outcome, and more risky. This makes them of great importance.

2 Tactical

Tactical decisions are concerned with short to medium-term objectives, and usually involve the implementation of strategic decisions and planning. The long-term risks are fewer and the significance, therefore, more moderate. However, as tactical decisions turn strategic decisions into reality, they are more likely to involve the great responsibility of overseeing and handling budgets, people, schedules, and resources.

3 Operational

Operational decisions are concerned with day-to-day systems and procedures, so tend to be more structured—to the extent that they can be routine or pre-programmed. As the third level down in the decision chain, they are used to support tactical decisions. The outcomes of operational decisions therefore tend to be immediate to short term, and involve few risks (although a series of wrong decisions will mount up and cause damage in the longer term).

Step two: Find the information you need

✔ Give yourself as much time as you can to research the background to a decision you need to make. As far as possible, try to resist the temptation to promise a quick decision.

✔ Identify the sources of information you will need and make sure they are near at hand. Get advice from experts or colleagues, and be honest about those areas where you do not have the answers.

✔ Wherever possible, cut out assumptions: check your facts. This might look like an extra hoop to jump through, but it is a valuable one. If you base a decision around a factor or number of factors that actually turn out to be unreliable, you'll have wasted hours of work anyway.

TOP TIP

Ask for help from your colleagues or manager
if time is very short, or you've reached an
impasse. A brainstorming session is often a
good idea, and often people who are new to an
issue may see a solution that you've
overlooked.

Six thinking hats

This powerful technique, developed by lateral thinking
pioneer, Edward de Bono, will help you to look at
decisions from many perspectives.

✓ Imagine that you have to wear a series of different
coloured hats, one after another, in order to look at an
issue from every angle.

■ White hats focus on the data, look for gaps,
extrapolate from history, and examine future trends.
■ Red hats use intuition and emotion to look at
problems.
■ Black hats look at the negative, and find reasons why
something may not work. If an idea can get through
this process, it's more likely to succeed.
■ Yellow hats think positively. This hat's optimistic view
helps you to see the benefits of a decision, providing a
boost to the thinking process.

- Green hats develop creative, freewheeling solutions. There is no room for criticism in this mode; it's strictly positive.
- Blue hats orchestrate the meeting—you're in control in this hat. Feel free to invite a new 'hat' to speak to keep ideas flowing.

Step three: Outline the alternatives and their consequences

✔ Get a few options for ways of dealing with an issue down in writing, then explore the positive and negative consequences of each. Give special attention to the unintended consequences that might arise, especially if you are considering a course of action that you have not tried before. You may find it useful to list these in columns alongside the options.

TOP TIP
Force field analysis is useful for examining pros and cons. By looking at the forces that will support or challenge a decision (such as finances or market conditions), you can strengthen the pros and diminish the cons. Draw three columns, and place the situation or issue in the middle. The pros push on one side, and the cons push on the other. Allocate

scores to each force to convey its potency. This allows you to measure the overall advantages and disadvantages of any given action. SWOT analysis is another handy grid technique that works by identifying the strengths and weaknesses of a decision, and examining the existing opportunities and threats. You can find more information on these techniques online (see 'Useful links' at the end of this chapter).

Step four: Judge each alternative by your goals

✔ Go back to what you wanted your decision to achieve; that is, remind yourself of what your priorities are in this situation. This forces you always to consider your longer-term goals when making your shorter-term decisions, and ensures that they are 'pointing in the same direction'.

✔ Measure the merits and problems of each alternative— this may be a case of estimating financial costs and benefits, or it may involve less tangible factors like goodwill or publicity. This involves a forward-thinking process of predicting what will happen as a result of your decision. Make a note of these expectations, as they will be important when you review your decision later on and judge with hindsight whether it was a good one.

✔ Compare the alternatives with each other, and decide which one comes out best in the light of the information available.

TOP TIP

Decision trees are a great way to help you examine alternative solutions and their impact, especially when decisions are required in situations where there is a great deal of information to sift through. Start your decision tree on one side of a piece of paper, with a symbol representing the decision to be made. Different lines representing various solutions open out like a fan from this nexus. Additional decisions or uncertainties that need to be resolved are indicated on these lines and, in turn, form the new decision point, from which yet more options fan out.

Step five: Take the decision, and implement it

✔ Make sure that everyone involved is informed about the decision you have taken; the value of a good decision is often undermined if your staff or colleagues hear about it through inappropriate channels. You will normally need to inform the more senior people first, but speed is often of the essence when letting people know. Plan your timing carefully and control the process firmly.

✔ Explain the reasons why the decision was made, especially if it is a contentious one. Outline what benefits you expect as a result, as well as any other implications that the business needs to anticipate.

✔ Get the right people onto the job of implementing the decision, so that it gets the best possible chance of success.

Step six: Review the consequences of your decision

✔ Decide how long it will take before the decision will have an effect, and plan an assessment at that time to review how well it went. Make sure that some measurement is being made that you can use later to help in your assessment. If it's a decision to send out a promotional mailing, for instance, then ensure that someone is collecting information on the impact of that mailing on daily orders.

The review should be a learning exercise—not just for you but for everyone concerned with making the decision and implementing it. Try to get as many of these people as possible involved in the review process. This will help them when a similar decision needs to be taken next time; it will also advance their own decision-making skills and enhance their value to the business.

Common mistakes

✗ You put off making a difficult decision

Procrastination will seldom lead to a decision becoming easier to make. Give the decision some thought as early as you can, and give yourself a deadline for making it— based on how long you think you need to gather the necessary information and input, and how important a decision it is.

✗ You make snap decisions under pressure

Making any decision without enough thought is risky; if you are in a pressurised office situation and time is short, there is the added danger of not being able to see the whole picture. In a quick decision, you may not give time to seeing important consequences of your actions.

✗ You don't consult those who will be affected

Nothing is quite as demotivating for staff as feeling as if their input is not valued or their feelings are not respected. Before you begin to address a decision, think carefully about each of the people who are—or could later be—affected by the outcome. Make sure that you include them—not necessarily all of them at every step, but leave them in no doubt that their input is appreciated.

✗ You let your bad decisions overshadow your good ones

No-one can get it right 100% of the time, and there are bound to be occasions when your decisions do not have the effect you'd hoped for or intended. Try not to be too downcast by this, and see bad decisions as part of the learning process, not as indications of failure. If you learn from a bad decision, that in itself is a good outcome. Don't be too hard on yourself.

STEPS TO SUCCESS

✔ Clarify why you want to take the decision, and what benefits you expect to flow from it.

✔ If others will be affected by the decision, get them involved in making it, to contribute information and alternative solutions.

✔ Consider using a range of established techniques like six thinking hats, force field analysis, decision trees, and SWOT analysis to help you cover all the options and assess their likely effectiveness.

✔ Plan what needs to be done in implementing the decision fully, so that everyone involved feels part of it.

✔ Make time to review the decision and make changes if the outcome is not what you had hoped.

Useful links

businessballs.com:

www.businessballs.com/problemsolving.htm

Mind Tools:

www.mindtools.com/pages/article/newTED_00.htm

Time Management Guide:

www.time-management-guide.com/decision-making-skills.html

Virtual Salt:

www.virtualsalt.com/crebook5.htm

Getting the best from virtual meetings

'Virtual' meetings—ones that are held without the participants being in the same room, or even the same country—are increasingly a popular option for businesses, especially global concerns. They allow teams of people who might never have the occasion to meet in person to 'get together' and share their news, views, and concerns. They also save a good deal of money that might otherwise be wasted on travel expenses and accommodation bills.

Not all business situations are suited to virtual meetings, but this chapter will explain how to get the best out of them if they're the solution you choose.

Step one: Think about whether the occasion suits a virtual meeting

For many business situations, such as a project team catch-up or discussions about a non-controversial subject, not having all the participants in the same place is not a problem. As long as you have an agenda (see below) and a clear idea of what you want to achieve, you should be able to move through most items painlessly.

Sometimes, however, meeting in person is much the better option. You may be better off with this route if, for example, you are:

- meeting an important customer or a potential customer
- trying to defuse a difficult situation
- concerned that language barriers may be a problem
- trying to persuade someone to fund your project

In all of these cases, it's likely that you will get a better result if people can see you in the flesh. Situations that are already tense can be made worse if the person you're speaking to can't see your body language or facial expressions—a light-hearted aside could go down like a lead balloon, for example.

Before you think about the virtual options open to you, think through all the implications carefully. One of the benefits of virtual meetings is that they are cost-effective, but in cases where the stakes are high, it may be worth investing in a business trip.

TOP TIP
If you need to demonstrate physically how something works—whether it be a piece of equipment or a software package—it's much better to be there in person rather than trying to communicate via an Internet or video connection. Not only can the other meeting participants get a much better view of what you are presenting, but they can ask

---

**questions or raise issues there and then
that might otherwise take weeks of
e-mails or phone calls to address.**

Step two: Think about the options open to you

The most popular and easily accessible form of virtual meetings is the teleconference. This service allows several people to all link into the same phone call, so that everyone can hear each other speak and contribute to the conversation. Teleconferencing is a low-cost way to bring together people based in different parts of the country, or indeed the world, and most telephones can support this service. If yours doesn't, a host of teleconference providers can be found online.

There are some drawbacks to this solution, though, including:

- **time differences.** Depending on where your participants are based, it may be hard to find a time that suits everyone.
- **no visual connection.** As the people taking part can't see each other, it may be hard to check that you are all referring to the same document, looking at the right version of a contract or specification, and so on.
- **everyone may talk at once.** Again, as you have no visual clues as to who is desperate to speak or who may

be boiling with rage, without careful control a teleconference may descend into a free-for-all where everyone speaks at once. Read on for advice on how to keep things on track.

TOP TIP

Whatever virtual meeting solution you use, remember not to feel 'bounced' into decisions: this can be a particular problem if you're discussing an issue over the phone. You may feel tempted to fill a (tactical) silence, say something you don't mean, or offer something that you're not absolutely sure will work in terms of logistics or costs, just to get the other person off the phone. Resist this, take your time, and if you feel harried, tell the other person that you will get back to him or her as soon as you can once you've done some investigations.

Video conferencing and its Internet counterpart, Web conferencing, are also popular options these days.

Video conferencing is the use of a live video link to connect people in different locations so that they can see and hear each other and conduct their meeting in real time. It's a useful tool for managing communication between remote workers, staff at geographically dispersed offices (including those who form a virtual team), or with clients at remote locations. It is also used in distance learning courses.

There are two basic options for video conferencing. The more expensive option is full-blown videoconferencing using ISDN lines, dedicated equipment, and large screens, which guarantee a higher quality experience. This can be expensive, though, as it will mean investing in all of the necessary equipment. Unless you hold video conferences regularly, you might choose to spend your budget on other things—particularly if your company is a small one.

TOP TIP

One option to investigate is the use of serviced offices which provide video-conferencing facilities. There are a range of companies offering this service and some can by rented by the hour or even the half hour, which might give you the flexibility you need. If you choose this route, it's more important than ever to circulate your agenda in advance and keep things moving so that you can book the room for the right amount of time and not feel pressurised into making decisions in a hurry. If you do feel that you need more time, either arrange another short meeting or talk through any final details by teleconference. If you are chairing the meeting, make sure all participants are kept informed of decisions.

Cheaper and more common is the PC/Web-based video conferencing which piggybacks on existing PC and Internet techonology and occupies a window on a PC. With Web conferencing the quality of transmission can vary, but it is improving all the time as an option, and can offer a range of useful tools including a virtual white board, shared access to documents, and so on.

As with videoconferencing, your business can use the services provided by a range of companies, including Webex and Microsoft, to get the best from online meetings. You can opt for a 'pay-as-you-go' solution, or sign up to a monthly or annual subscription if that would suit you best.

Step three: Prepare as you would for any other meeting

Just because the participants aren't all in the same room doesn't mean that you can get by without preparing for the meeting. You still need to come away from it with some decisions taken, and you're much more likely to do that if you have spent time thinking about what you want to get out of it.

If you're chairing a virtual meeting, once you know that all participants can make the day and the time you suggest:

- prepare and circulate an agenda well in advance
- remind everyone the day before the meeting of the time you have agreed and double-check that they are comfortable with the technology involved

- set some ground rules at the outset so that everyone knows what to expect and how to get the best from the time you have (see below for more advice on how to achieve this)
- sum up key points regularly

TOP TIP
If you're taking part in a teleconference and you work in an open-plan office, it might be worth trying to find a spare meeting room in which you can take the call. This means that your colleagues won't be disturbed if you need to speak more loudly than normal, and that you can lay out all relevant paperwork in plenty of space rather than be confined to your desk.

Step four: Lay some ground rules

Even in face-to-face meetings, the chair needs to run through a few 'housekeeping' rules so that everyone is aware of basic arrangements. In virtual meetings, these are even more useful as they can make the difference between a useful and well-ordered session and a confusing exchange of ideas.

- Ask everyone to introduce themselves at the beginning of the meeting and, if you are the chair, check that everyone you are expecting is there.

- Explain that only one person should speak at any one time and that the person speaking should not be interrupted.
- Be more proactive than you would normally about tackling unfocused comments. If you're not sure who the speaker is addressing, ask him or her if their comment was directed at anyone in particular.

TOP TIP

Do be tactful if you need to intercede in this way. Watch your tone carefully so that the speaker doesn't feel under attack. Sarcasm or irony don't tend to come across very well when other people can't see your facial expression or body language, so you need to strike a balance between seeking clarification for the good of the meeting and seeming as if you have no sense of humour. Tread lightly and keep your intonation upbeat and positive.

- Be patient with participants whose first language isn't the same as yours. Even if they have good English, it may take them a little while to get up to speed with native speakers, so ask everyone to speak clearly and slowly as the meeting gets under way.
- Don't take silence as agreement. In some types of virtual meeting, there may be a time delay if telephone lines or Internet connections aren't ideal, so make sure you give each participant time to contribute. In some cases, the relevant connections may have broken down altogether,

so it is a good idea to sum up regularly, asking each participant to acknowledge their assent with what has been decided.

■ Make plans at the end of the meeting for the next time you need to meet (virtually or face to face), if appropriate. It will save a lot of time if everyone can confirm their availability when you are all together.

■ Thank everyone for their participation.

TOP TIP

Again, make sure you follow up with a note of all decisions agreed. Most people see meetings as a chore, and will stop contributing or taking part if they feel that nothing ever happens as a result. If you're the person responsible for co-ordinating the outcomes of a meeting, sum up decisions promptly, making a note of who is doing what and what the relevant deadlines are.

Common mistakes

✗ You 'multitask' in the background

Just because other people can't see what you're doing doesn't mean that they won't realise quickly if you're not paying attention. You may think that you can answer your e-mails (quietly), address some envelopes, or make tea while still participating fully in a teleconference, but you can't. Treat virtual meetings as you would any other type and give everyone your full attention.

✗ You don't think you need an agenda

Like face-to-face meetings, virtual meetings need an agenda to keep everyone on track and—hopefully—on time. Everyone's time is precious, so if you are in charge of organising or chairing a virtual meeting, make sure you get an agenda round to all participants well in advance. If you're a participant and you haven't received one the day before the meeting, ask the chair to send one along to you.

STEPS TO SUCCESS

✓ Virtual meetings are a useful way of speaking to colleagues or clients who you may normally not have the opportunity—or the funds—to meet in person.

✓ They are more appropriate for some types of meeting than others, though, so think carefully about whether a virtual meeting is the best solution. If you are meeting an important customer, seeking funds, trying to defuse a difficult situation, or physically demonstrating how something works, it is probably better to meet in person.

✓ There are three main ways of holding a virtual meeting: teleconferencing, video conferencing, and Web conferencing.

✓ Teleconferencing is the simplest and most cost-effective solution. The main drawback is that you have no visual 'clues' to how other participants are feeling—body language can communicate a huge amount about someone's real reaction to something—and also it's harder to check that you're all looking at the same paperwork.

✔ Remember to 'rein in' a teleconference, so that only one person is speaking at once.

✔ Video and Web conferencing options mean that you can actually see the other people you're speaking to, but the quality of the picture may vary depending on the bandwidth of your computer systems.

✔ Don't worry if you don't have the budget to invest in costly equipment: many companies now offer 'pay-as-you-go' options or fully-equipped suites that you can rent by the hour or half hour when you are holding your meeting.

✔ Whichever virtual meeting option you choose, treat it with respect. Pay full attention as you would do at a face-to-face meeting.

✔ If you're chairing a virtual meeting, prepare for it fully. Once you know the preferred date, circulate an agenda well ahead of time and make sure that everyone is comfortable with the technology being used.

✔ Set some ground rules so that everyone can benefit from the meeting: for example, make clear that only one person should speak at once.

✔ Sum up decisions regularly throughout the meeting and write up the minutes promptly, making clear who is expected to do what, and when.

Useful links

Microsoft:

www.microsoft.co.uk

Webex:

www.webex.co.uk

Running a brainstorming session

In the main, meetings are held to discuss a tightly-defined list of issues. You might, for example, need to discuss marketing plans for a new product or service, finalise a budget, or confirm a schedule.

On other occasions, however, you might be right at the other end of the life cycle of a product or service and might need to come up with:

- an idea for the product in the first place
- a name
- a strapline
- potential collaborators

Alternatively, you may just have a tricky problem that you want to share with others. In any of these situations, a brainstorming session could be just what you need. The words 'brainstorming' and 'meeting' may sound like a contradiction in terms, since creativity requires time and meetings usually restrict it, but it is possible to manage this balancing act. This chapter looks at ways of allowing people the freedom to let their thoughts run riot, while at the same time harnessing that creativity into something genuinely useful.

Step one: Be clear about what you want to achieve

Even though the joy of brainstorming is that it allows people to 'freewheel' and be creative in the way they think about things, it will only be an effective means of tackling a problem if you are very specific about what you want to achieve. This doesn't mean you should suggest a potential outcome (see the box below) as this would set limits on the participants' ideas even before you start, but do be sure of what your overall goal is and roughly how you want to get there. Don't forget to set a time limit.

Brainstorming or analysis?

Before you go too far down the brainstorming route, do make sure that this is the right way to tackle your problem. Brainstorming is best done when you need to innovate and create a range of ideas. If you already have some possible solutions to a problem but just don't know which one to pick, it's probably best to hold an analysing session, in which you work out the pros and cons of each solution separately. Brainstorming may simply confuse the issue by producing even more potential solutions, none of which are more compelling than those you have already identified.

TOP TIP
You can, of course, brainstorm from scratch.
You might have to do this if you want to
move into a completely new area of business,
for example. However, it might be more
productive to do some research beforehand,
so that you are aware of what potential
competitors are doing in that field.

Step two: Find the right mix of people

First of all, be sure that you're the right person to be leading the meeting (often called a 'facilitator'). Good facilitators have the right mix of enthusiasm, knowledge, tact, and team-leading skills to make sure that the brainstorming group is pulling together during the session. Don't be afraid to ask a colleague to step in and facilitate if you think you might not be the best person for this job: sometimes, in fact, it might be helpful to have someone with some distance from the issue under discussion, as they'll be able to be more objective.

You might also find it useful to ask a wider variety of people to attend than you would for a standard meeting. Obviously you will need people there who know your business, department, or team well, but think carefully about other colleagues or contacts who—even though they might not work on your projects every day—can bring their talents or experience to bear on the issue being discussed.

TOP TIP

Some people are natural problem solvers, others can think up snappy headlines in an instant, while others might have first-hand experience of the issue you are facing. Tap into the talent in your business and benefit from it. Remember that most people are flattered to be asked for their help. It's always better not to expect too much, though: if someone can give you an hour, don't try and stretch it to two. And always say thank you!

Step three: Pick the right place and time

Finding the right time of day to hold your brainstorming meeting can be tricky as people reach their 'peaks' at different times of the day. Some aren't at their best early in the morning, for example, while others know that their energy flags in the early afternoon. Holding the meetings before lunch is no bad idea, however, as you can use it as a natural break and it will give everyone something to aim for.

TOP TIP

If you think the meeting may go on for some time, do schedule in short breaks for refreshments along the way. This will also give people a chance to check their

**messages and so on; if they are worried
about missing an important call, they'll
be preoccupied with that rather
than the issue being discussed.**

Good venues for brainstorming are well-lit, spacious rooms
that allow the participants to move round comfortably. Other
useful considerations are as follows:

✔ Try to find a room that is quiet, and that you can close the
door on so other colleagues aren't disturbed. If your
budget stretches to hiring a room outside your normal
office building, so much the better—it will help foster
the idea that you're trying to get away from established
thinking and procedures.

✔ Make sure you have a whiteboard and plenty of paper
and pens so that ideas can be noted.

✔ Keep the atmosphere as informal as you can by avoiding
rigid seating plans; if you need a table in the room, try to
get a round one so that no-one's seated at the head of it.

✔ Ask everyone to turn off their mobile phones so that they
won't be disturbed during the meeting.

Step four: Stay flexible

At the beginning of the meeting, clarify again just what it
is that you're brainstorming so that everyone is up to speed.

This first part of the session is the one when you are throwing the issue open to everyone's differing creative approaches, so stay flexible and don't dismiss any idea out of hand.

As the facilitator:

✔ Make sure everyone joins in.

✔ Don't criticise suggestions that you think are outlandish: not only will you dampen the mood of the meeting, but you'll risk dismissing what could be (after some development) the very idea that gets you the ideal solution—or on the way to it.

✔ Make a note of all suggestions on the whiteboard, flip chart, or large pieces of paper you're using to record potential solutions; having these clearly visible around the room will help spark off other ideas.

✔ More is definitely best at this stage: encourage everyone to come up with as many ideas as they possibly can.

TOP TIP
Try to keep the momentum up during this phase of the brainstorming by being actively enthusiastic and positive. If you sense that energy is flagging, give people a measurable but eminently achievable goal: 'let's think of five more ideas before we break for lunch', for example.

As the session draws to a close, thank everyone for their time and collaboration and let them know what will happen next. If you'd like them to read over the minutes so you can start isolating the best ideas, tell them when you expect these to be ready and stick to that date.

TOP TIP

Ideally, you'll have delegated the minute-taking to someone else. This is much the best option, but if you *do* end up doing it, write up the notes from the meeting as soon as you can. The longer you leave it, the more likely it is that they'll make no sense!

Step five: Whittle down the ideas into a practical solution

Now that you have your list of ideas, you need to rank them in order of practicality. Will any of them really work in the cold light of day? If you are asking the brainstorming team from the meeting to help you evaluate the ideas, ask them to plump for their top five (maximum) ideas, rejecting those that are just too off the wall.

Once you have compiled a 'master' top five list, look at each option carefully, working out:

■ costs
■ time scales

- competition
- legal issues
- negative factors

TOP TIP
If the project under discussion or potential solutions are controversial or would represent a radical change of direction for the company, it is worth talking them through as soon as you can with senior decision makers. If the final decision rests with you, fine, but if not, you'll need to get everyone onside as early as possible so that you can address any issues promptly.

Common mistakes

✗ You don't do a reality check

If you're chairing or facilitating the brainstorming session, do remember that even if an idea is exciting, it might not necessarily be useful! Organisations looking for a unique product or service may be tempted to pick up on ideas that—while they have a good immediate impact—really have very little mileage in them. It's important to have a reality check to make sure that only those ideas that are viable actually end up on the market. If the timing or context is wrong, there is a danger that big, often expensive, mistakes will be made.

✗ You're not receptive enough to new ideas

Sometimes the most obvious ideas are dismissed because they threaten the status quo or challenge long-held, never-questioned values. Bottled water is a good example. It was launched at a time when drinking water was considered to be a commodity that should be freely available to all. However, what originally seemed like a commercial non-starter has turned into a major sector of the soft drinks market. Always ask yourself: on what basis am I rejecting this idea? It might be the next bottled water!

STEPS TO SUCCESS

✔ Brainstorming is an excellent way to tap into your colleagues' creativity so that you can find new ideas.

✔ If you already have some solutions to a potential problem, brainstorming probably isn't the best way forward. In this case, you need to analyse all options carefully rather than generate new ones. See Chapter 5 for more advice on good decision-making.

✔ Even though one of the joys of brainstorming is being able to 'freewheel' and come up with innovative ideas, you must be very specific about your goal at the outset, or you won't get any practical results at the end.

✔ Find the right mix of people to get the best results. You need an enthusiastic facilitator who can harness everyone's creativity, as well as a team made up of people from all over the business who can add their own perspectives to the mix.

✓ People who don't work with you directly are always good team members for brainstorming, as they are able to be more objective.

✓ Pick the right place and time for the meeting. A well-lit, comfortable venue will be conducive to comfortable creativity.

✓ The first part of successful brainstorming is to get the team to come up with as many ideas as possible. Stay flexible and don't reject anything at this stage, however unusual it might be.

✓ Keep up the momentum of the meeting by watching out for anyone who seems to be flagging.

✓ Delegate the job of taking minutes to someone else if at all possible. If you can't, write up the minutes of the meeting as soon as you can so that the ideas stay fresh in your mind.

✓ This stage is the one in which to evaluate all ideas, draw up a shortlist and investigate each one thoroughly in terms of cost, competition, time scale, and any potential negative aspects.

✓ Discuss any potentially controversial decisions with your manager if you're not the person who can take the final decision.

Useful links

Brainstorming.co.uk:
www.brainstorming.co.uk
Businessballs:
www.businessballs.com

Where to find more help

101 Ways to Make Meetings Active: Surefire Ideas to Engage Your Group
Mel Silberman
San Francisco, California: Jossey-Bass Wiley, 1999
336pp ISBN: 0787946079

This book provides 101 tools, tips, and techniques for successful meetings. The topics that the author covers include preparing for meetings, obtaining group participation, stimulating discussion, the roles and responsibilities of chairpersons and other officers, timesavers, managing conflict, problem solving, using flip charts, and closing the meeting. All are illustrated with a number of practical examples.

The Big Book of Business Games
John Newstrom, Edward Scannell
Maidenhead: McGraw-Hill, 1995
170pp ISBN: 0070464766

Designed for managers and team leaders, this book lists 75 games and activities to enliven meetings and inspire productivity. Taken originally from the 'Games Trainers Play' series, each entry has been adjusted for use in a range of business situations.

The Definitive Book of Body Language: How to Read Others' Attitudes by Their Gestures
Allan Pease
London: Orion, 2005
400pp ISBN: 0752858785

Being able to interpret other people's body language will give you a great insight into what they *really* feel about something or someone. This book claims to help you 'learn to read other people's thoughts by their gestures'. Once you know the basics, you'll be able to use this knowledge to your advantage in all areas of life, including working out if someone is lying, and how to get others to co-operate with you.

First Aid for Meetings: Quick Fixes and Major Repairs for Running Effective Meetings
Charlie Hawkins
Newberg, Oregon: Bookpartners Inc, 1997
190pp ISBN: 1885221614

This book provides concrete ideas for running effective meetings, including planning, managing the flow of the meeting, moving groups to consensus and closure, and dealing with disruptive behaviour. The author also discusses how to manage meetings in which electronic media are being used and how to apply meeting management concepts to one-to-one meetings.

Getting Results from Electronic Meetings: Creative Solutions, Increased Commitment, Improved Business Processes
Alan Weatherall, Jay Nunamaker
Chandlers Ford: Electronic Meetings Solutions Ltd, 1999
192pp ISBN: 095265251X

Electronic meetings have already established an impressive track record for helping organisations to exploit existing common technology in ways that bring about immediate and quantifiable business benefits. This book describes in a clear and logical way how electronic meetings can be practically implemented in any organisation.

Getting to Yes
Roger Fisher, William Ury, Bruce Patton
London: Random House Business Books, 2003
224pp ISBN: 1844131467

By working around four main principles of effective negotiation and discussing the difficulties that can arise, the authors show the reader how to pursue his or her own interests while keeping adversaries happy at the same time. A few principles will guide the reader no matter what the other side does, or whatever what tricks they may resort to.

Manipulating Meetings: How to Get What You Want When You Want it
David Martin
Harlow: Prentice Hall, 2000
206pp (Smarter Solutions Series)
ISBN: 0273645005

This practical and readable guide identifies the best and most successful techniques for enabling managers to achieve their objectives at meetings. The issues covered include: deciding if your meeting is really necessary; chairing and controlling meetings effectively; and composing dynamic agendas. Practical advice is given on dealing with time wasters, ambushes, and bullies, while putting your point across and getting your own way.

Not Another Meeting! A Practical Guide for Facilitating Effective Meetings 2nd ed
Frances A. Micale
Central Point, Oregon: PSI Research, 2002
160pp ISBN: 1555716326

This manual discusses the importance of being able to distinguish content from process, how to encourage participation, how to stay 'in the moment' during a meeting, how to resolve conflict, and how to make the best use of teams in meetings.